'Corgarff Castle', drawn about 1790 by C. Cordiner.
courtesy of the Royal Commission on the Ancient and Historical Monuments of S...

Corgarff Castle stands close by the A939
at Cock Bridge in Upper Strathdon

CORGARFF CASTLE

Iain MacIvor and Chris Tabraham

EDITED BY CHRIS TABRAHAM
ILLUSTRATED BY DAVID SIMON
PHOTOGRAPHY BY HISTORIC SCOTLAND PHOTOGRAPHIC UNIT
PRODUCED BY ROY STEWART PRINT SERVICES
PRINTED IN SCOTLAND FROM SUSTAINABLE MATERIAL
BY BUCCLEUCH PRINTERS LTD., HAWICK

FIRST PUBLISHED BY HISTORIC SCOTLAND 1993
REPRINTED 2003
CROWN COPYRIGHT © HISTORIC SCOTLAND 1993
ISBN 0 7480 0659 1

INTRODUCTION

"Gi' up your house, ye fair lady,
Gi' up your house to me,
Or I sall burn yoursel therein,
Bot and your babies three."

(FROM THE BALLAD *EDOM O' GORDON* RECOUNTING THE
BURNING OF CORGARFF IN NOVEMBER 1571)

Corgarff is no run-of-the-mill castle, though the visitor might be led into thinking this on first seeing the building in its lonely moorland setting. The impression that Corgarff is something a little out-of-the-ordinary is confirmed as the visitor draws near and makes out more clearly the star-shaped perimeter wall surrounding the little tower.

Corgarff's story is in fact two stories. The first episode takes us from the middle of the sixteenth century, when the tower was built, through to the closing years of the seventeenth century, when it seems to have been abandoned. This was the castle's heyday, during which time it served as the impressive fortified home of the laird of Corgarff. It was also the scene of a most horrific tragedy, the burning of the tower and its twenty or more occupants in the winter of 1571.

Many tower houses were seen as old-fashioned by the 1700s and Corgarff would probably have been left to decay had it not been for its important strategic position in this remote district during the troubled days that followed the flight into exile in 1688 of the last of the Stuart kings, James VII of Scotland. Temporarily occupied by Jacobite troops during the '15 and '45 Risings, Corgarff was requisitioned by Government forces after the Battle of Culloden in 1746 and the castle began its second life as soldiers' barracks. By 1750 the old medieval tower had been transformed into an acceptable garrison outpost.

Although the military threat which brought the Redcoats to Upper Strathdon soon evaporated, the soldiers continued to occupy the place while they supported the revenue officers in stamping out the illegal production and smuggling of whisky. They finally withdrew in 1831.

Corgarff Castle shortly after the garrison moved out in 1831, painted by James Giles.
(Courtesy of the National Trust for Scotland.)

THE STORY OF CORGARFF CASTLE

THE SEAT OF THE FORBESES OF TOWIE

The castle at Corgarff in Upper Strathdon was erected about the middle of the sixteenth century. The builder's identity is unclear. The 'Forest of Corgarff' had been granted by James IV to Alexander Elphinstone (residing at Kildrummy Castle and later created the first Lord Elphinstone) in 1507, and the second Lord Elphinstone made over the estate to his eldest son as a marriage gift in 1546. Perhaps the erection of the tower followed this happy event.

Shortly after the marriage, however, the lands of Corgarff were passed to a tenant of Lord Elphinstone's, John Forbes of Towie, and it is equally possible that he was responsible for the castle on the hill. Strathdon was then one of the most wild and remote districts of Scotland and the Forbeses would have required a strong house to protect themselves, their dependants and valuables.

In style and plan the castle was typical of contemporary small houses of the gentry being built throughout the country. The nucleus of the castle was the tower house. Above a basement for storage was the main room, the hall. The upper floors contained private chambers and a garret. Around the courtyard beside the tower were other buildings, including a stable, bakehouse and brewhouse, all enclosed within a stone perimeter wall.

THE HORRIFIC TRAGEDY OF 1571

The castle's eventful history in the mainstream of Scotland's story began in 1571. In that year the cause of the deposed Mary Queen of Scots was being upheld by, amongst others, Adam Gordon of Auchindoun, brother of the Earl of Huntly. The Forbeses of Corgarff were allied with the opposing party, which supported Mary's son James VI.

In November 1571, Adam Gordon's men came to Corgarff intent on taking the castle for Queen Mary. The laird himself was away but Margaret Forbes, his wife, refused them entry. And so the assailants savagely set the castle on fire and Margaret, her family and servants, were burnt to death. In all about 24 people died. The tragedy is remembered in the ballad *Edom o' Gordon*.

Artist's impression of Corgarff Castle as it might have looked about 1550.
(Drawn by Dave Pollock.)

CORGARFF AND THE JACOBITES

Life in the countryside around Corgarff in the seventeenth century continued to be dangerous and violent. In 1607 Corgarff was seized and held by a band of local ruffians supported by 'Highland thieves'. Two years later a group of Highlanders attacked the stockmen and shepherds of Corgarff and stole their animals.

In 1645 the castle figured once more in national affairs when it was occupied by the Marquis of Montrose, campaigning on behalf of Charles I. In the Rising of 1689-90, it was burnt by the Jacobite supporters of the exiled James VII to deny its use as a garrison post to the forces of William of Orange.

By now the castle was owned by the Earl of Mar who, launching the Jacobite Rising of 1715 from his ancestral castle of Kildrummy further down the glen, marched to Corgarff to recruit and arm his forces before going on to Braemar to raise the standard of James VIII (the 'Old Pretender').

This incident illustrates Corgarff's peculiar importance. Though fortified, it was certainly no major place of strength; but its secluded position made it an ideal base for fomenting disaffection, which the established government found it difficult to counter.

CORGARFF AND THE '45

Corgarff's remoteness was emphasised during the Jacobite Rising of 1745-6. In the spring of 1746, the army of Prince Charles Edward (son of the 'Old Pretender') had retired in good order from Derby in the English Midlands to the Scottish Highlands. Whilst the Duke of Cumberland advanced slowly up the east coast, the Jacobites established a magazine of powder, muskets and ammunition at Corgarff, preparing for a lengthy war of movement in the mountains.

A raid by 300 infantry and 100 cavalry, commanded by Lord Ancram, was launched from Aberdeen. The arduous progress of the detachment through bitter weather and snowstorms is described in a letter from one of the officers with the party:

"(after) a most terrible march...we found it abandoned by the Garrison, but so lately, that the fire was burning...and no living creature in the house but a poor cat sitting by the fire."

The task of destroying the military stores, begun by the Jacobites before they fled, was completed by the Redcoats. Shortly after, on 16 April 1746, the Jacobite army itself was defeated at the Battle of Culloden.

Kildrummy Castle in Strathdon, 13 miles east of Corgarff, from where the sixth Earl of Mar launched the '15 Jacobite Rising.

CORGARFF AND THE REDCOATS

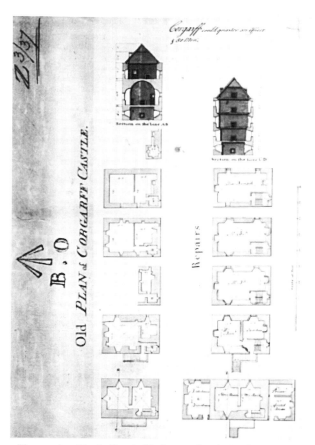

Plans produced by the Board of Ordnance after the '45 Jacobite Rising for the conversion of Corgarff Castle into soldiers' barracks. (Courtesy of the National Library of Scotland.)

After Culloden the military authorities decided to include western Aberdeenshire in its network of garrisons. By 1748 work was in hand to convert the castles at Corgarff and Braemar into soldiers' barracks, while a new military road running from Blairgowrie in the south to the new fortress at Fort George on the Moray Firth was planned to pass close by both places. Braemar became the main military station under a captain, with Corgarff's garrison headed by a subaltern. (A date - 1748 - and several sets of initials carved on a fireplace lintel on the third floor were recorded in the 1920s but are scarcely visible now.)

In 1750 Ensign Robert Rutherford, serving in General Pulteney's Regiment, the 13th Foot, was at Corgarff in command of a detachment of 45 non-commissioned officers and men from Fort George. About half were outposted, either living in hired barns or billeted on a reluctant and frequently hostile local population. A sergeant, a corporal and 21 men remained quartered in the castle along with their senior officer.

Corgarff Castle from the south west. The low pavilions on either side of the tower house and the star-shaped perimeter wall, with its musket slits, were added about 1748.

The tense atmosphere in the glen in those early days of the garrison is reflected in Ensign Rutherford's reports. In one report, dated October 12, 1750, he writes:

"One of the soldiers ...had his fingers cut very desperately by a fellow in the country on wednesday last, the soldier says it was because he would not drink the pretender's [that is, Bonnie Prince Charlie's] *health, but the fellow denies that, however I sent a party, and had him apprehended at night, and he was sent to justice of peace who has order'd him to find bail to stand his trial on monday next."*

This extreme animosity does not seem to have prevailed for long. By 1754, Major-General Bland, Commander-in-Chief of George II's forces in Scotland, felt able to write:

"Brae Mar and Corgarff, where we now have two small barracks erected, the good effects of which is now plainly felt by bringing in the people of that barbarous and mountainous country into a peacable and orderly state, and they are now become honest and industrious and live with great friendship and amity with His Majesty's troops quartered there."

The birth of Nathaniel Forbes at Corgarff Castle on 2nd February 1766 (his memorial can be seen in Strathdon Kirk) suggests that life in the garrison was not too difficult.

Memorial tablet in Strathdon Kirk to Nathaniel Forbes, born at Corgarff Castle in 1766.
(Courtesy of Guy Paget.)

CORGARFF AND THE EXCISE

Redcoats remained at Corgarff long after the Highlands had ceased to pose a military threat to the established government. By the end of the eighteenth century, the castle's military importance had faded, with a garrison of two or three Invalids (soldiers disabled on active service or too old to serve in the field) outposted from the Company of Invalids stationed at Fort George. The castle was even used as a shooting-lodge on occasions.

In 1802 the castle was returned to private hands. A local man, James McHardy,

The still-room in the west pavilion of Corgarff Castle, reconstructed in 1989.

rented it as a farmhouse, and in 1826 even held a licence permitting him legally to distil whisky on the premises. But in the following year he was removed when the army again took possession, this time in support of the excisemen then engaged in a countrywide campaign to stamp out the time-honoured illicit pro-duction and smuggling of the 'mountain dew'. Save your sympathy for Farmer McHardy: he became the garrison's main supplier of provisions, and at prices which reflect a seller's market!

The garrison now comprised a captain, a subaltern and fifty-six men from the 25th Regiment of Foot who, until 1831, assisted the revenue officers. As the larger garrison could not be accommodated within the tower, a nearby cottage was rented from Mr McHardy to provide space for the barrack-sergeant and a small hospital. This was replaced by a purpose-built structure in 1829.

THE TWILIGHT YEARS

When the garrison pulled out in 1831 most whisky in Scotland was, for the first time, being produced with the approval of Government and the excise – after a long battle against the good old days which the soldiers at Corgarff had helped to win. For more than a century afterwards the castle fell slowly into decay. At first it was occupied by farm labourers, but it became derelict after the First World War. With its roofs fast falling into ruin, Corgarff was given into State care in 1961 by Sir Edmund and Lady Stockdale, who subsequently assisted in the first phase of preservation work.

Corgarff as a ruin shortly before it came into State care in 1961. The restoration work received an award in 1976.

The Castle Ladies.

The last residents of Corgarff Castle - the Ross sisters - sitting outside the west pavilion in 1912.
(Courtesy of Guy Paget.)

A SHORT TOUR OF

1. PERIMETER WALL
A STAR-SHAPED DEFENSIVE WALL, LOOP-HOLED FOR MUSKETS, BUILT BY THE MILITARY IN 1748. THE LITTLE BARRACKS AT CORGARFF WAS DESIGNED TO HOLD ITS OWN AGAINST LIMITED HOSTILITIES BUT NOT AGAINST ATTACK BY ARTILLERY.

2. CISTERN
A SHALLOW TANK PROVIDING A WATER SUPPLY FOR THE GARRISON.

3. COURTYARD
AN OPEN AREA AROUND THE TOWER HOUSE DURING THE MILITARY OCCUPATION, BUT FORMERLY THE SITE OF NUMEROUS CASTLE BUILDINGS (EG, STABLES, BAKEHOUSE, BREWHOUSE), SURROUNDED BY A WALL OF MORE STRAIGHTFORWARD PLAN.

4. EAST PAVILION
ADDED TO THE TOWER HOUSE IN 1748 TO PROVIDE A GUARD ROOM AND PRISON CELL. ALTERED IN 1827 TO PROVIDE A POWDER MAGAZINE.

5. WEST PAVILION
ADDED TO THE TOWER HOUSE IN 1748 TO PROVIDE A BREWHOUSE FOR THE GARRISON. CONVERTED INTO A SMALL DISTILLERY IN THE 1820s BY THE LOCAL FARMER, MR McHARDY, AND IN 1827 MADE INTO A KITCHEN AND BAKEHOUSE FOR THE NEW GARRISON.

6. TOWER HOUSE
BUILT ABOUT 1550 AS THE RESIDENCE OF THE FORBES LAIRD OF CORGARFF. CONVERTED INTO SOLDIERS' BARRACKS IN 1748 AND ABANDONED FOR MILITARY USE IN 1831.

7. ENTRANCE
THE ONLY ENTRANCE INTO THE TOWER HOUSE, AT FIRST-FLOOR LEVEL. NOTE THE PROJECTING CORBEL STONES AT THE TOP OF THE TOWER DIRECTLY OVER THE ENTRANCE, THE REMAINS OF A DEFENSIVE DEVICE CALLED A MACHICOLATION. THIS HAD BEEN ABANDONED BY 1748.

CORGARFF CASTLE

Artist's bird's-eye view of the castle from the south west.

LIFE AT CORGARFF

A LORDLY RESIDENCE

Corgarff Castle was built as a lordly residence about the middle of the sixteenth century. Despite the sweeping changes made to the tower by the military authorities between 1748 and 1750, enough survives in the building to indicate how it was intended to be used as a residence by the laird during its early years. And what does not survive in the fabric has survived in measured drawings made in 1748 by the Board of Ordnance, who had responsibility for all military building and construction work at that date.

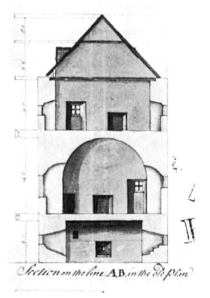

Section on the line A.B. in the old plan

A section through the old tower house showing the arrangement of the accommodation, particularly the high stone-vaulted hall on the first floor, from a Board of Ordnance plan of 1748.
(Courtesy of the National Library of Scotland.)

The rectangular tower house was modest in size, measuring some 12 m by 8 m and standing to a height of almost 15 m. It had four principal floors, arranged in the conventional manner for the period - storage in the basement; hall on the first floor; private chambers above. The floors were linked by a stone spiral stair which was in the same position as the present timber stair, the south-east corner. A stone newel (an upright column around which the steps spiralled) from that stair is visible in the south wall of the first-floor room.

The basement was divided into two stone-vaulted **cellars**, both of them cool and dimly lit through narrow slits. They housed the main provisions for the lord and his family, though there would have been further storage space in buildings outside the tower.

The first floor contained two unequal-sized rooms. The larger room was the **hall**, the main living space in the tower. With its high stone-vaulted ceiling, generous windows, and good-sized fireplace in the end wall, the hall must have presented quite an imposing spectacle in its day.

A cut-open reconstruction of the tower house showing how the interior may have been used about 1600.

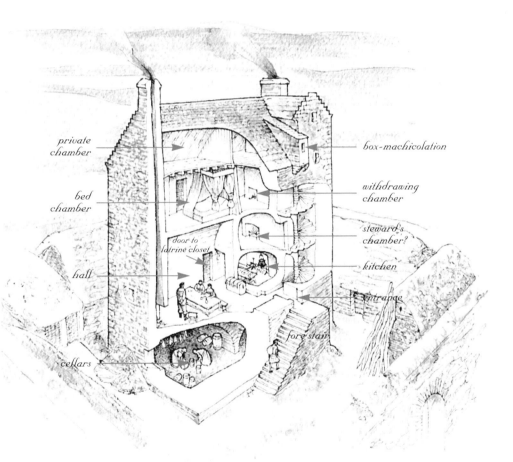

private
chamber

box-machicolation

bed
chamber

withdrawing
chamber

door to
latrine closet

steward's
chamber?

hall

kitchen

entrance

fore stair

cellars

The smaller room served as the **kitchen** and originally had a large fireplace in the end wall. The room was also covered by a stone vault, though not so lofty as that over the hall because directly over the kitchen was a little room, likewise stone vaulted, with a small fireplace, two wall cupboards and a latrine closet in one corner. This little room may have been the **private chamber** of the laird's steward.

The third floor was taken up by two rooms more or less of equal size. Each had a fireplace and what appear to have been latrine closets in their north walls. These rooms formed the laird's private suite, comprising his **withdrawing chamber** and **bed chamber**. The three rooms at the top, one of them a little cap-house at the head of the stone stair, provided further **private chambers** for the laird's family and household.

As for defensive arrangement, the tower was certainly provided with a small overhanging defence, called a **box machicolation**, right over the entrance doorway from where those within could defend the door, the weakest part of the castle. The projecting stone corbels supporting this machicolation are still visible.

The tower never stood alone, but from the outset would have been surrounded by other buildings – stables and other service rooms – grouped around a courtyard. None has survived, but the reference in a Board of Ordnance plan dated 1748 to two huts abutting the tower confirms the presence of other structures. No doubt these were all contained within a defensive courtyard wall.

The box-machicolation over the entrance doorway.

SOLDIERS' BARRACKS

The work undertaken by the Board of Ordnance between 1748 and 1750 saw the 200-year old tower converted into soldiers' barracks.

The basement alone remained largely unaltered, the **two cellars** continuing in use as stores for food, drink and military supplies. The rest of the tower was completely gutted. The most radical change was the complete removal of the stone-vaulted ceiling over the lofty hall and the insertion of an extra floor. The resulting space provided sleeping accommodation for the commanding officer, three NCOs and 42 men.

The first floor contained the **officer's room** and a kitchen. Here lived Lieutenant Moody in 1749, Lieutenant Leslie and Ensign Rutherford in 1750, and their successors in this isolated command. The room served as their bedroom, sitting-room and office. Here they wrote regular returns and reports to their senior officer at Braemar Castle, issued orders to their subordinates and interviewed any Highlander arrested on suspicion of supporting the Jacobite cause, or for wearing Highland dress, or for illegally distilling or smuggling whisky. The room would have been simply but fairly comfortably furnished, in contrast to the rudely-finished and overcrowded barrack rooms on the upper floors.

The **kitchen** was converted, probably in 1827, into an apartment for a second officer. A new kitchen was then made in one of the pavilions which had been built in 1748 flanking the tower.

One of the barrack rooms in Corgarff Castle, reconstructed in 1989.

The upper floors were **barrack rooms**, though the poorly lit topmost floor was probably reserve accommodation. Contemporary drawings show a crowded maximum provision of eight double beds to each room, though only five or six would have been needed for the two NCOs and 23 men serving there in 1750. The NCOs, one to each barrack room, had a bed to themselves; the privates slept two to a bed.

Ancillary accommodation was provided in two flanking single-storey pavilions. The **west pavilion** contained the bakehouse and brewhouse. A soldier's basic diet was made up of bread and beer. Both staples were made here and rationed out daily to the men. In addition, each man received a pound of beef a day, only occasionally supplemented with cheese, butter or peas. The beef was generally of inferior quality and the weight included bone and gristle! The men cooked for themselves, either in the garrison kitchen or over the grates in their barrack rooms, where they also ate.

The men baked their own bread or oatcakes in the oven provided, but the beer was made by a brewer contracted to come in weekly with his assistant to maintain the stock. In addition to his daily ration, each man could buy extra, but with his daily pay of 12d and beer at 2d a pint there was not much room for luxuries.

A reconstruction of a Redcoat firing through one of the musket loops of the perimeter wall. The cistern holding the garrison's water supply is in the foreground.

Corgarff Castle from the north.

The **east pavilion** contained the guardroom and prison. The main function of the garrison was to police the remote glens of west Aberdeenshire, searching out Jacobite sympathisers or anyone found contravening the law that prohibited wearing of Highland dress. Even at this early date the Redcoats were instructed to stamp out the illegal distilling and smuggling of whisky. All prisoners were held in the cell until they could be escorted under guard to magistrates in Aberdeen or Perth. The magistrate available to the military at Inverness was scarcely used, as experience had shown that he rarely upheld a prosecution; his sympathies were too much with his fellow Highlanders.

When the army reoccupied the barracks in 1827, the east pavilion was altered to provide a powder magazine whilst the west pavilion became the garrison kitchen and bakehouse.

The cobbled **courtyard** about the tower and pavilions was enclosed by a **star-shaped wall** loop-holed for musketry. The little barracks were designed to be held against limited hostilities, but not against attack by artillery. So far as we can tell, they were never put to the test.

THE MILITARY ROAD NEAR CORGARFF

The military road linking the mighty Highland garrison fortress - Fort George - on the Moray Firth with Blairgowrie and the Lowlands, built between 1749 and 1753, passes close by Corgarff Castle. A length of the military road can be walked for about 3 miles (5 km), leaving the A939 about 1 km east of Corgarff Castle and continuing south east.

An effective road network was seen by General George Wade as critical to the successful pacification of the Highland clans. Soon after his arrival in Scotland as Commander-in-Chief in 1724, he set in train a massive road-building programme. By the time of his departure fifteen years later, there were over 250 miles of road winding and twisting through the mountains and glens, replacing the tracks of earlier times. Thereafter his assistant, Major William Caulfield, took over, building three times as many miles of road and assisting with advice to many county officials then engaged in building roads in order to encourage economic growth.

Invercauld Bridge, over the River Dee, completed in 1753.

An inscription at the Well of the Lecht, north of Corgarff. The road at this point is still in use as the A939.

These military roads were greatly appreciated – not least by Prince Charles Edward's army during the '45 Rising. That network, responsibility for which passed in 1814 to the Commissioners appointed under the terms of the Road and Bridges Act of 1812, forms the basis of the modern road system in the Highlands. Many stretches, like that running past Corgarff (now the A93 and A939), are still in use, and some of the bridges, notably the Invercauld Bridge over the River Dee north of Braemar, are beautiful reminders of their fine work.

The roads were built largely by the soldiers, with specialists from the Board of Ordnance carrying out the survey work and stone-masons contructing the bridges. The work was carried out in the summer season by gangs of up to 500 men, who received double pay for their aches and pains. They were quartered under canvas, in huts and temporary barracks, retiring to permanent quarters for the winter.

A rock-breaking party during road construction about 1750, by Paul Sandby.
(Courtesy of the National Galleries of Scotland.)

FURTHER PLACES TO VISIT

Corgarff Castle is one of a number of ancient monuments associated with the Jacobite Risings of the eighteenth century which are in the care of Historic Scotland and well worth a visit. They include:

FORT GEORGE (11 miles NE of Inverness by the village of Ardersier)
One of the outstanding fortifications in the British Isles. Planned after the Battle of Culloden in 1746 as an impregnable base for George II's army, and completed in 1769. Continues to serve as an army barracks but with its full complement of original garrison buildings and encircling artillery defences still intact.

Fort George

RUTHVEN BARRACKS (near Kingussie)
An infantry barracks built after the 1715 Jacobite Rising, with stables added by General Wade in 1734. Captured by Prince Charles Edward's army early in 1746. Here the remnant of that force gathered shortly after its defeat at Culloden.

Ruthven Barracks

INVERCAULD BRIDGE (near Braemar)
The most impressive of the military bridges built along the route of the Blairgowrie - Fort George military road between 1749 and 1754. The greater part of that road is still in use as the A93 and A939.

KILDRUMMY CASTLE (13 miles E of Corgarff)
The mighty thirteenth-century castle of the Earls of Mar, where in the summer of 1715 the sixth Earl of Mar finalised his plan for a Rising in support of the exiled James Stuart, the 'Old Pretender'.

FURTHER READING

ON CORGARFF CASTLE:
W Simpson 'Corgarff Castle, Aberdeenshire',
Proceedings of the Society of Antiquaries of Scotland, 61 (1926-7), 48-103
W Simpson *The Earldom of Mar* (1949)

ON SCOTTISH CASTLES GENERALLY:
S Cruden *The Scottish Castle* (1981)
C Tabraham *Scottish Castles and Fortifications* (1990)
C Tabraham and D Grove *Fortress Scotland and the Jacobites* (1995)
C Tabraham *Scotland's Castles* (1997)

ON MILITARY ROADS:
J Salmond *Wade in Scotland* (1938)
W Taylor *The Military Roads in Scotland* (1976)